MASTER THIS!

D0864767

Guitar

Seb Wesson

ESSEX CC LIBRARIES
30130 168024981

First published in 2009 by Wayland
This paperback edition published in 2011 by Wayland

Copyright © Wayland 2009

Hachette Children's Books
338 Euston Road
London NW1 3BH

Wayland Australia
Level 17/207 Kent Street
Sydney NSW 2000

All rights reserved.

Senior editor: Claire Shanahan
Produced by Tall Tree Ltd
Editor, Tall Tree: Jon Richards
Designer: Jonathan Vipond

British Library Cataloguing in Publication Data
Wesson, Seb.
Guitar. -- (Master this)
1. Guitar--Juvenile literature. 2. Guitar--Methods--Juvenile.
I. Title II. Series
787.8'7193-dc22

ISBN: 9780750265478

Printed in China

Wayland is a division of Hachette Children's Books, an Hachette UK company.

www.hachette.co.uk

Picture credits
All photographs taken by Michael Wicks, except;
t-top, b-bottom, l-left, r-right, c-centre
2 Dreamstime.com/Vladislav Lebedinskiy, 5t Stephen Hiird/Reuters/Corbis, 5b Dreamstime.com/Nexus7, 6l Dreamstime.com/Vladislav Lebedinskiy, 7l Dreamstime.com/Magomed Magomedagaev, 7r Dreamstime.com/Duane Ellison, 8tr Dreamstime.com/Robert Spriggs, 8bl Corbis, 9b Dreamstime.com/Andrea Leone, 13tl Dreamstimecom/Magda Moiola, 15tr Tim Wimborne/Reuters/Corbis, 17br Michael Ochs Archives/Corbis, 26tr Joe Giron/Corbis, 28 Josh Armstrong/The Christian Science Monitor via Getty Images, 29t istockphoto.com

The website addresses (URLs) included in this book were valid at the time of going to press. However, because of the nature of the Internet, it is possible that some addresses may have changed, or sites may have changed or closed down since publication. While the author and publisher regret any inconvenience this may cause the readers, no responsibility for any such changes can be accepted by either the author or the publisher.

Disclaimer
In preparation of this book, all due care has been exercised with regard to the advice, activities and techniques depicted. The publishers regret that they can accept no liability for any loss or injury sustained. When learning a new activity, it is important to get expert tuition and to follow a manufacturer's instructions.

Acknowledgements
The publishers would like to thank Chad Brown, Lucy Pisapia and Tom Jordan for their help with this book.

Contents

Playing the guitar 4
Types of guitar 6
Other equipment 8
Holding the guitar 10
Chords and strumming 12
Scales and picking 14
Staves and rhythms 16
The musical alphabet 18
Special effects 20
Rhythm and chord skills 22
Advanced techniques 24
Putting it together 26
Taking it further 28
Glossary and further information 30
Index 32

Playing the guitar

The guitar is one of the most exciting musical instruments you can learn to play. It works wonderfully when it is played with someone who is singing or other instruments, or when it is played as a solo instrument.

Played by all

The guitar can be played in a wide range of musical styles, or genres, from classical to rock to jazz. Anyone can learn to play the guitar at any age, whether they are left- or right-handed. The positions described in this book are for right-handed players – you will need to reverse them if you are left-handed.

Mastering the guitar takes a lot of practice as it requires a great deal of coordination between your left and right hands.

*Mastering the guitar can pave the way to some exciting experiences. Here, Dave Grohl of the Foo Fighters plays a guitar **solo** in front of a huge crowd during a concert at Wembley, London, in 2007.*

Guitar heroes

There are many famous rock and pop guitar players. Eric Clapton and Jimi Hendrix popularised blues and rock guitar in the 1960s. Eric Clapton is still performing today to enormous crowds around the world. Brian May from Queen and Eddie Van Halen from Van Halen took rock guitar into the 1970s and 1980s, while bands such as Green Day and the Foo Fighters have brought guitar playing into the 21st century. All these bands and players have different musical styles and use the guitar in different ways.

History

Musical instruments similar to the guitar have been around for more than 5,000 years. However, different numbers of strings were used in instruments, such as the **oud** with 11 strings. The modern, six-stringed classical guitar first appeared in Seville, Spain, in the 1850s.

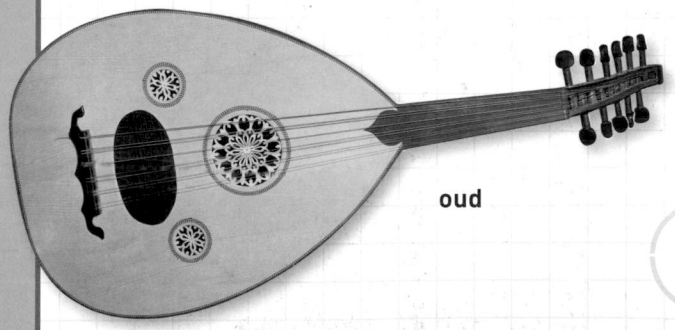

oud

Types of guitar

There are two types of guitar used in modern music; the **acoustic** guitar and the electric guitar. Although the principles and techniques of playing them are the same, they can be used to create very different sounds.

Vibrating strings

All guitars have strings that are plucked to make them **vibrate**. This vibrating produces the notes. Most guitars have six strings, each of a different thickness. The thinner the string, the higher the note it produces. You can also change the **pitch** of a note, by placing your fingers on the fretboard.

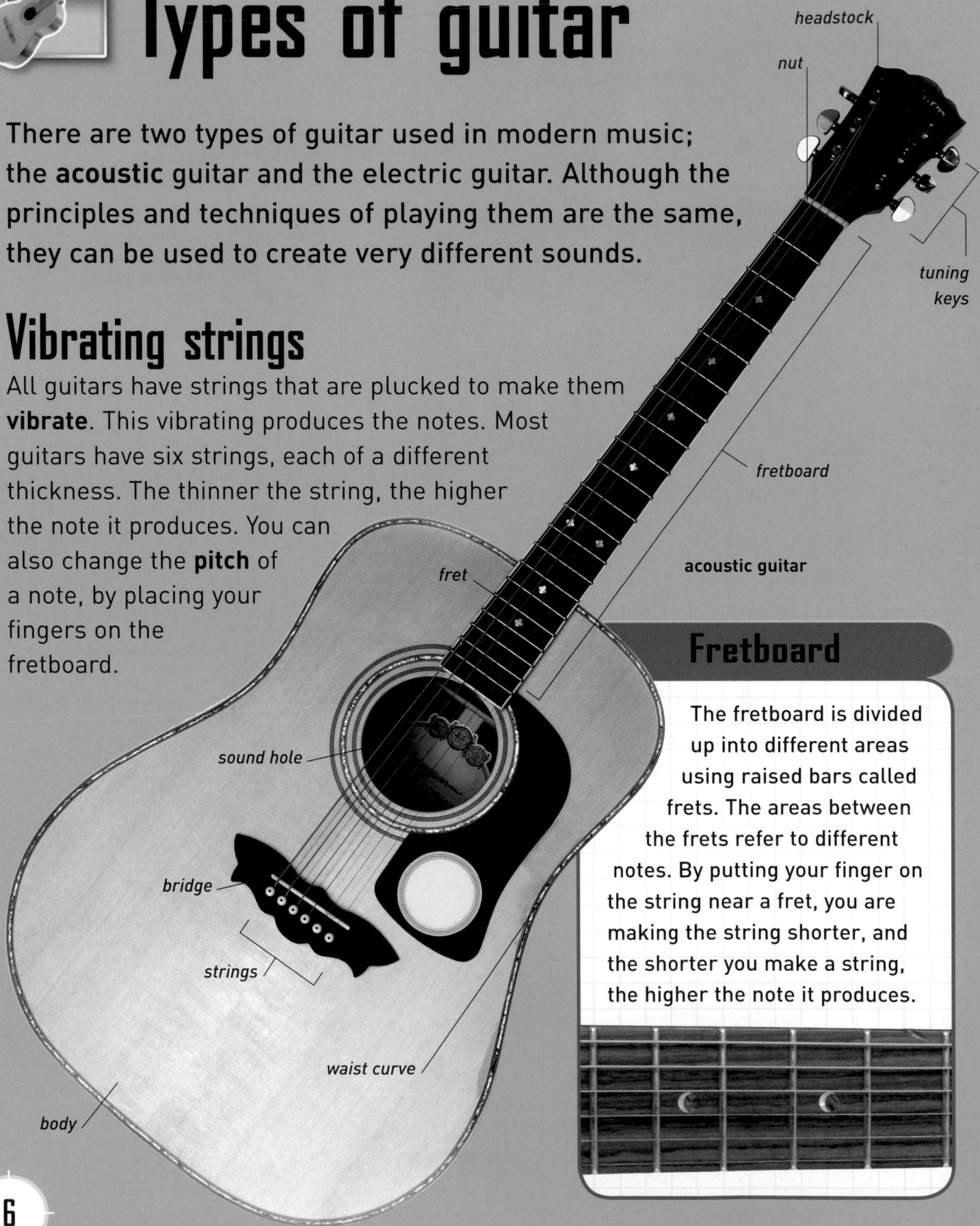

acoustic guitar

Fretboard

The fretboard is divided up into different areas using raised bars called frets. The areas between the frets refer to different notes. By putting your finger on the string near a fret, you are making the string shorter, and the shorter you make a string, the higher the note it produces.

Making it louder

Electric and acoustic guitars differ in how they **amplify** the notes, or make them louder. Acoustic guitars have a large, hollow body. The air inside the body vibrates with the strings, making the notes louder when they come out of the sound hole. Electric guitars have electric **pickups** which detect the vibrations of the strings (see below).

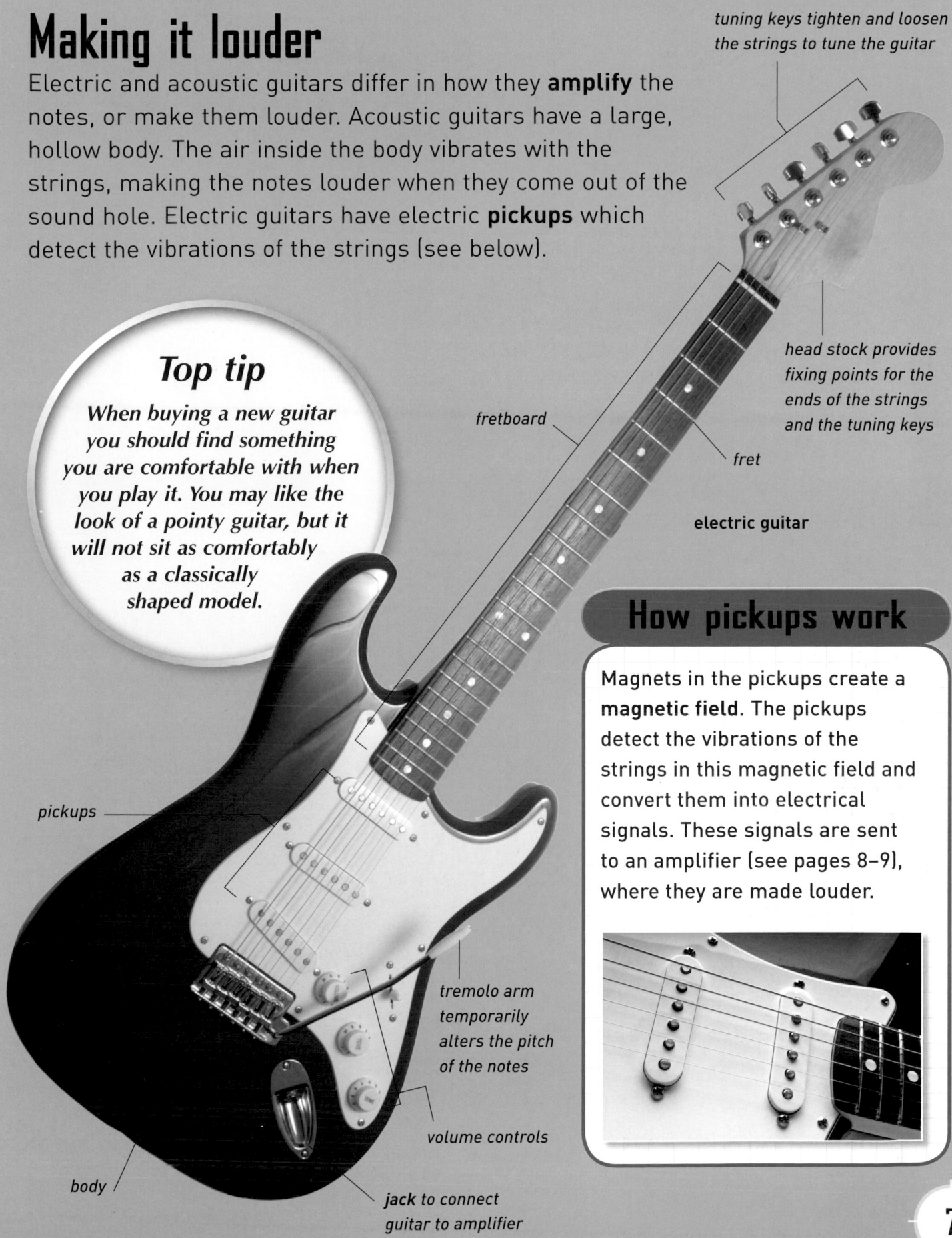

electric guitar

Top tip

When buying a new guitar you should find something you are comfortable with when you play it. You may like the look of a pointy guitar, but it will not sit as comfortably as a classically shaped model.

How pickups work

Magnets in the pickups create a **magnetic field**. The pickups detect the vibrations of the strings in this magnetic field and convert them into electrical signals. These signals are sent to an amplifier (see pages 8–9), where they are made louder.

Other equipment

In addition to the guitar itself, there are a few other pieces of equipment you will need. This equipment will help you tune, hold, amplify and strum your guitar properly.

Bits and pieces

A guitar strap is essential when playing in live situations as it will help you to hold the guitar while standing up (see pages 10–11). It should be adjustable so that it holds your guitar at the correct height. If you are sitting down to play, then a foot rest will raise your foot and stop the guitar from slipping off, while a music stand will hold any sheet music at eye level.

Star file

JIMI HENDRIX
Guitar genius

Jimi Hendrix was born on 27 November 1942 in the United States of America (USA). He played blues and rock mainly, writing famous songs such as *The Wind Cries Mary* and *Purple Haze*. He is recognised as a guitar genius who was way ahead of his time technically – even playing the guitar with his teeth at some concerts.

Using a plectrum

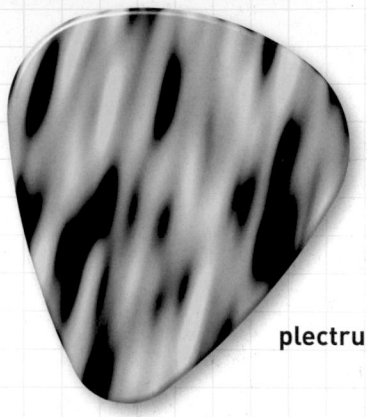

plectrum

Plectrums are used to pick the strings. They come in a variety of thicknesses, but usually, you should use a thinner plectrum for strumming chords and a thicker one for playing a tune.

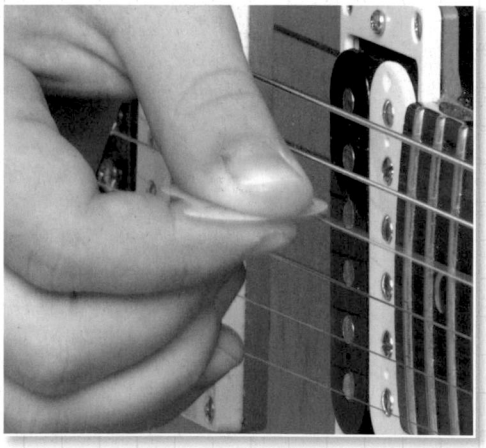

Hold the plectrum between the first finger and thumb of your strumming hand – if you are right-handed, this is your right hand.

Amplifier

The amplifier, or amp, contains electronic parts and a speaker that amplify, or make louder, the sounds from your electric guitar. You will also need leads to carry signals from the guitar output jack to the amplifier or to an electric guitar tuner (see below). These leads do not carry electricity to power the guitar and amp, but they carry the electrical signals created by the pickups (see pages 6–7).

Amps allow you to control the volume of the notes, making them louder or quieter. They also allow you to control how much ***bass*** *and* ***treble*** *your guitar sounds make.*

Electric tuner

An electric tuner detects the vibrations of each string and shows you whether that string is playing the right note (in tune) or not. You can then turn the tuning keys (see page 7) on the guitar to tighten or loosen the string to tune it (see page 17).

Holding the guitar

You can play the guitar sitting down or standing up. In general, acoustic music is played in a sitting position, while electric music, such as rock and pop, is played standing up, using a strap.

right arm should rest on top of the guitar's body

left hand should support the guitar's neck

When sitting to play an acoustic guitar, the waist curve of the guitar should rest on your right thigh.

legs should be level and not slope towards the floor

Sitting

Guitarists who play classical music tend to keep their legs wider while holding the guitar neck higher.

Standing

A good height to position your guitar when standing is a little lower than you would have it in the sitting position. Start in a sitting position and stand up holding the guitar where it is. You can then see how much you need to loosen or tighten your strap. Some guitarists, such as Slash from Guns and Roses, hold the guitar very low, while others, such as Johnny Borel from Razorlight, hold it much higher. There is no set way to hold your guitar – just do what works best for you.

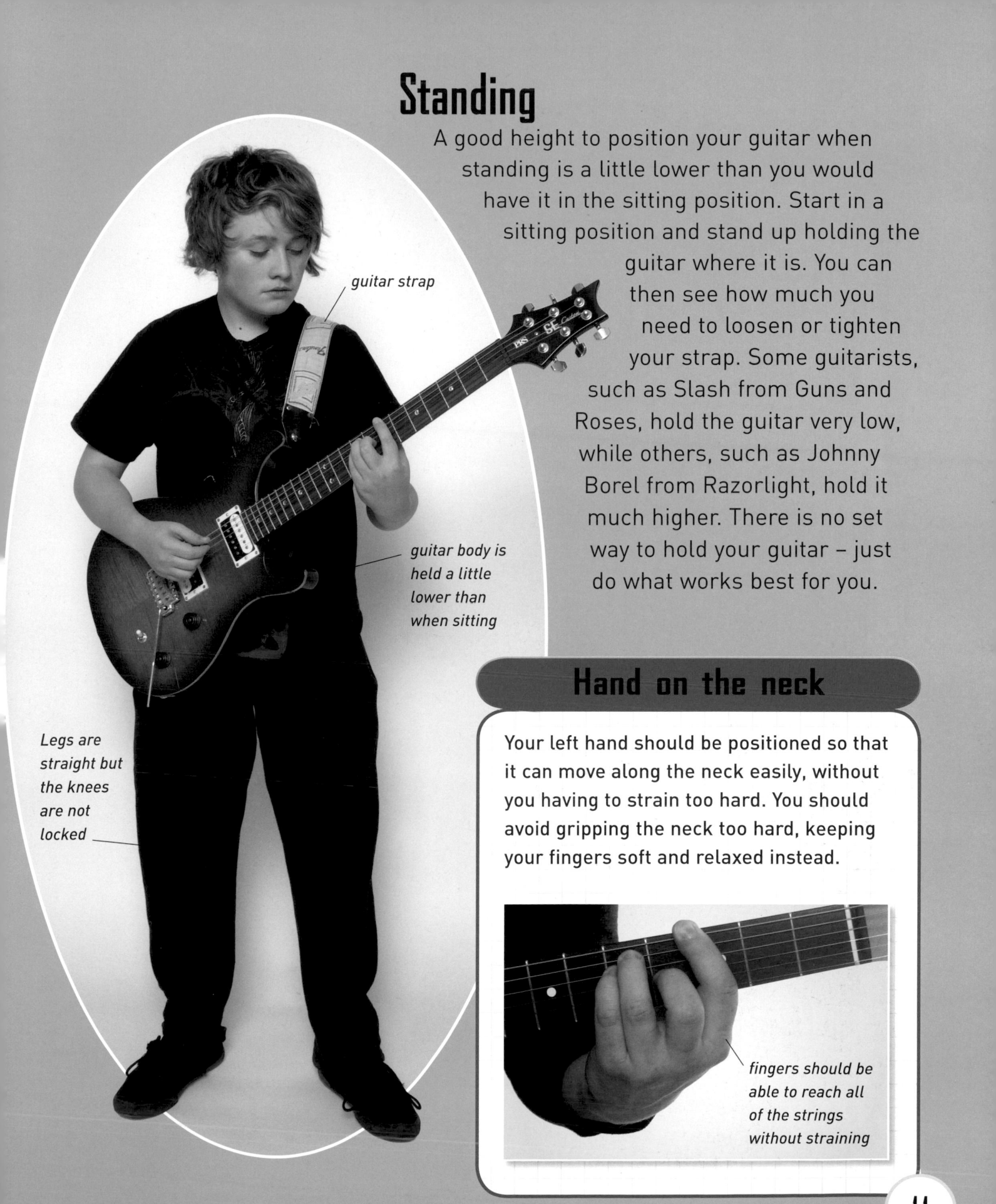

Hand on the neck

Your left hand should be positioned so that it can move along the neck easily, without you having to strain too hard. You should avoid gripping the neck too hard, keeping your fingers soft and relaxed instead.

Chords and strumming

A major part of playing the guitar includes playing chords. A chord is a group of notes that is played together at the same time.

To sound a note correctly you should put your finger on the string next to the relevant fret. Here, a guitarist has put his index finger up against a fret of the thickest string.

Finger work

The individual notes of the chord are made by positioning the finger tips of the left hand on the fretboard in the correct positions. When placing the fingers on the fretboard, it is important that they are close to the relevant fret, otherwise they will not sound the note correctly. The right hand can then strum all or some of the strings to sound the notes.

Strumming techniques

To strum the first chord, the hand holding the plectrum is held above the thickest string.

The hand is brought down quickly so that it hits, or plucks, each of the strings on the way down.

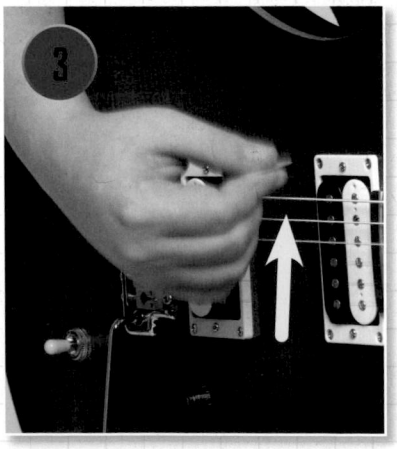

To play the next chord, the plectrum hand is brought upwards, plucking each of the strings again.

The guitar's six strings each have their own note. The thickest string plays the lowest-sounding note, and the thinnest string the highest. The strings, from the thickest to the thinnest, play the following notes, E, A, D, G, B, E.

Setting the mood

Chords can really set the mood of what you are playing, depending on what **key** they are in. For example, if the music is in a **major** key, then the chord may sound happy, but if it is a **minor** key, it can sound sad. Chords are used to create a musical layer in a song, over which a solo instrument will be played or a **vocalist** will sing. Chords can even be broken down into an arpeggio. This is when the notes of a chord are played one after the other, instead of at the same time (see pages 22–23).

Chord boxes

A chord box is a way of writing down a chord to show how it is played on the guitar. At the top there is an '0' to show that the string should be played without any fingers on a fret – this is known as 'open' – or an 'X' to show that you should not play that string (see the chords on page 19).

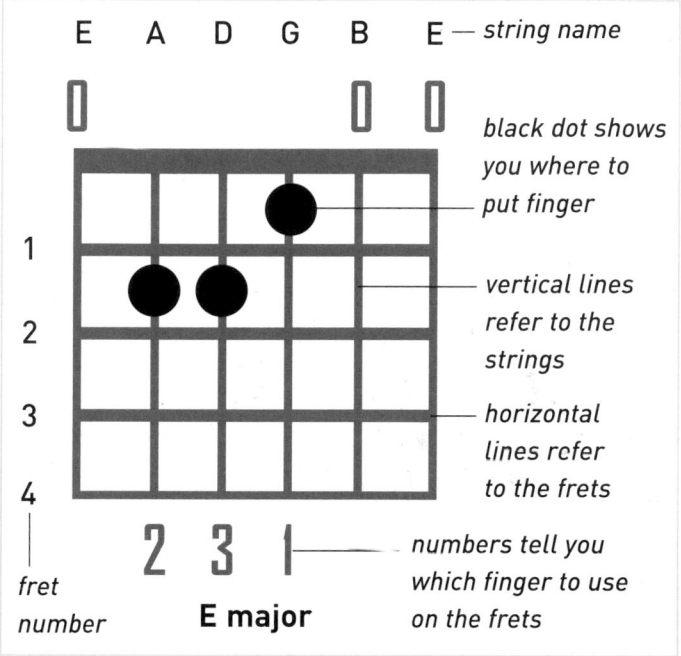

These are the finger positions for the chord box shown above. The fingers of the fret hand are numbered from one for the index finger to four for the little finger.

Scales and picking

Scales are individual notes arranged in order from the lowest note to the highest and back down again. Scales are used for many things in music, such as exercises to warm up your fingers. You will also find that most tunes are based on scales.

Top tip

You should change the strings on your guitar regularly to stop them breaking or rusting. Your guitar teacher can show you how to replace them.

One at a time

Unlike chords, where all the notes are played at the same time, notes in a scale are played one at a time, using a technique called alternate picking. This involves striking the string down for the first note, then upwards for the second note, then down for the next note, and so on.

Alternate picking

Hold the plectrum above the string you wish to pick and then strike it downwards to play the first note.

Bring the plectrum upwards to pick the string and change the finger position on the frets to play a note with a different pitch.

Playing tabs

Guitar tablature, or tab for short, is a simple way of recording information for guitarists. You can use it to read scales and chords as well as complete pieces of music, without having to learn how to read musical notation (see pages 16–19).

Tabs use a system of lines for the strings and numbers to show which fret the fingers should be placed on (see below).

Star file

THE EDGE
Rock legend

David Evans, also known as The Edge, is part of Irish rock band U2. He is famous for his simple tunes, or melodies, and distinctive chiming guitar sound, which he creates using special sound effects. He has played with U2 since they formed 30 years ago, creating rock classics such as *City of Blinding Lights* and *Vertigo*.

How to read guitar tabs

The top line represents the thinnest string, which plays the highest note, and the bottom line represents the thickest string, which plays the lowest note. The letters on the side represent the names of the notes of each of the strings (see page 13). The numbers that appear on the strings represent the frets you should hold down. As with the chord box, '0' means that the string should be played 'open', with no fingers on a fret.

Guitarists read the tabs from left to right, playing the fret indicated by the first number before moving onto the next number to the right, and so on. The guitar tabs featured here are for the scales C major and A minor.

letters represent string notes — *horizontal lines represent strings* — *numbers indicate which fret to play*

```
e|-----------------------|
b|--------------0-1------|
g|----------0-2----------|
d|---0-2-3---------------|
a|-3-----------------------|
e|-----------------------|
```

C major

```
e|-----------------------|
b|-----------------------|
g|--------------0-2------|
d|--------0-2-3----------|
a|-0-2-3-----------------|
e|-----------------------|
```

A minor

Staves and rhythms

As well as using guitar tablature and chord boxes, you can read music using musical notation. This is a system of dots that are positioned on a group of lines called a stave.

The stave

You can remember the line notes of the treble clef with the phrase 'Every Green Bus Drives Fast', while the space notes spell out the word 'FACE'.

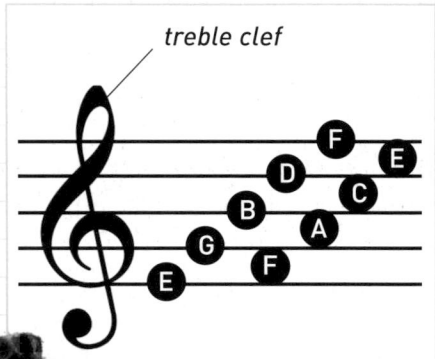

Guitar music

At the start of each line of music is a symbol called a **clef**. This shows you how high or low the notes on the stave are to be played. There are several different clefs, but music for the guitar is written using the treble clef. This means that the notes on the lines of the stave are, from lowest-pitched to highest, E, G, B, D and F. The spaces on the treble clef stave are, from lowest to highest, F, A, C and E. Put together, the notes make up the entire musical alphabet (see pages 18–19) using the letters A to G. Notes above or below the stave sit on small lines known as ledger lines.

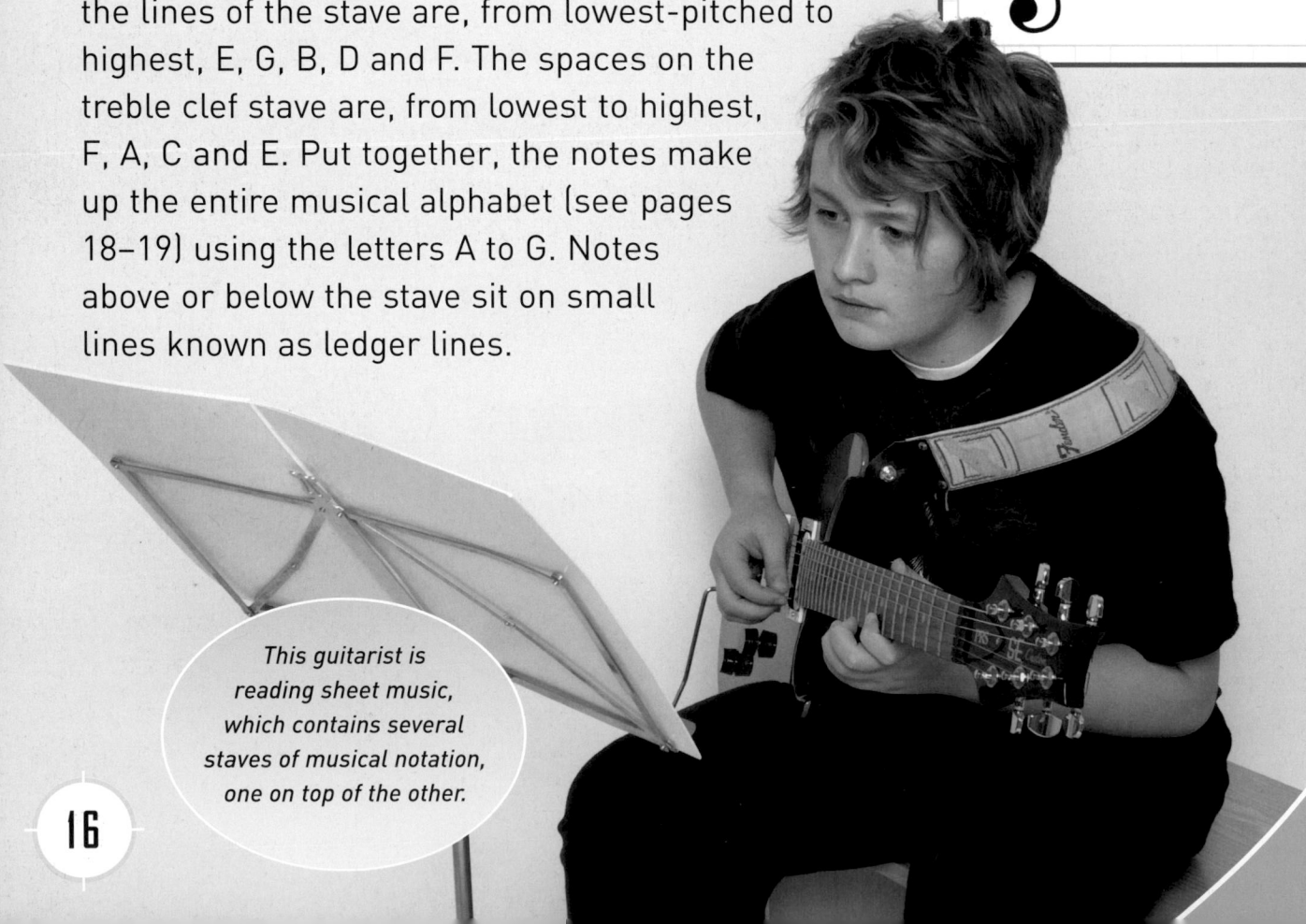

This guitarist is reading sheet music, which contains several staves of musical notation, one on top of the other.

Rhythms

As well as the notes and pitches, you need to know the right **rhythms** in order to play a piece of music. Music is divided up into bars, and a simple bar of music usually contains four beats. These beats are called **crotchets** and one beat equals one crotchet. The number of beats in a bar is shown by the **time signature**, which consists of two numbers that are written just after the clef.

Bar beats

In this case, there are four crotchets in a bar, as shown by the 'four-four' time signature. Each bar is divided by a barline. Different symbols are used to show notes of different lengths. For example, two crotchets, or beats, equal a **minim**, and two minims equal a **semibreve**.

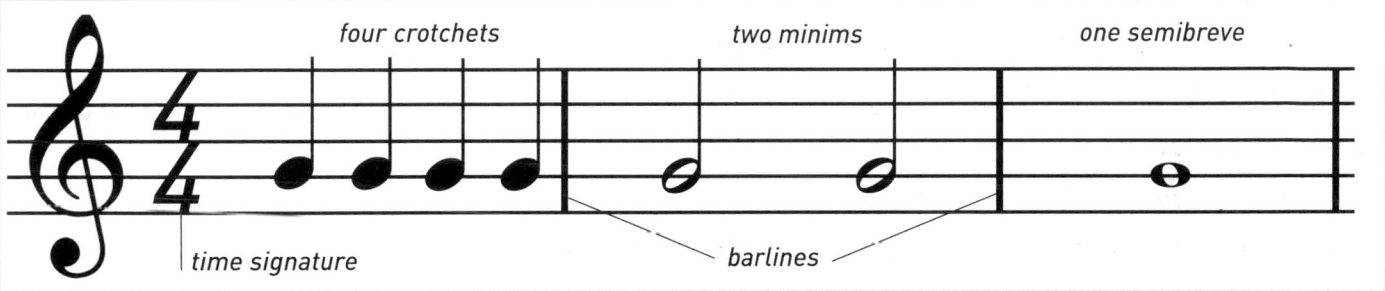

Tuning

To tune the guitar strings so that they play the correct notes, you can either use an electric guitar tuner (see page 9) or you can use your ear. Play the fifth fret of the thickest string (E) and it will sound the note that the string next to it should play (A). Tighten or loosen that string until it plays the same note. You can work up the guitar strings in this way, always playing the fifth fret of the string before the one you want to tune. One exception is the G string, where you have to play the fourth fret to sound the right note.

Star file

DJANGO REINHARDT
Gypsy master

Django Reinhardt was born in France on the 23 January 1910. As a young man his hand was injured in a fire and this prevented him from using two of his fingers on the fretboard. However, this did not stop him from developing an amazingly fast playing technique. He went on to invent the lively style of guitar music known as gypsy jazz.

The musical alphabet

As you play higher and higher pitched notes, the letters in the musical alphabet are repeated again and again. The jump from one A to the next A (or any other two notes with the same letter) is called an **octave**.

Sharps and flats

Each octave jump is split up into eight notes and in between most of these notes, there are other notes that are known as sharps (#) and flats (b). The gap between two notes is called an **interval**, and the smallest interval used in music, for example from A to A#, is a **semitone**. An interval of two semitones, from A to B, is called a **tone**.

Notes and frets

The entire musical alphabet, with all the sharps and flats looks like this: A-A#(Bb)-B-C-C#(Db)-E-F-F#(Gb)-G-G#(Ab)-A. You will notice that a sharp note is the same as the flattened note above it. For example, A# is the same note as Bb. Also, B-C and E-F do not have sharps or flats between them because they are a semitone apart. Below is an entire octave of notes, written out as musical notation and as a guitar tab. You will see on the tab that as you play one fret higher, the note rises a semitone.

Musical notation

```
e|-----------------------------0--1--2----3---4----5|
b|---------0--1--2-----3--4-------------------------|
g|2---3-----------------------------------------------|
d|-----------------------------------------------------|
a|-----------------------------------------------------|
e|-----------------------------------------------------|
```

Guitar tab version

Using the notes

Major and minor scales are formed by putting together specific sequences of tones and semitones. A major scale uses a certain sequence of tones and semitones. These are: root (starting note and key), tone, tone, semitone, tone, tone, tone, semitone. Using the musical alphabet and starting on the note A, you will get the A major scale and it should look like this:
A-B-C#-D-E-F#-G#-A.

Minor scales use a differenl sequence by lowering the third and sixth notes of the scale by a semitone. So an A minor scale would read:
A-B-C-D-E-F-G#-A.

Top tip

To help you visualise the intervals between each of the notes, look at the keyboard of a piano. There are thinner black keys for the sharps and flats between all of the notes except B–C and E–F.

Making chords

You can also use scales to make chords. Playing the first, third and fifth notes from a major scale will give you a major chord. For example, in A major that would be A-C#-E. Playing the first, third and fifth notes of a minor scale will give you a minor chord (A-C-E).

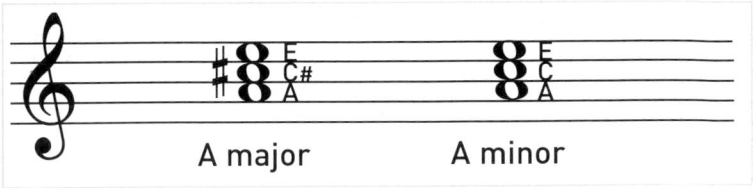

In musical notation, the notes of a chord are written above each other, as shown here. Now compare these with the chord boxes and photos shown below.

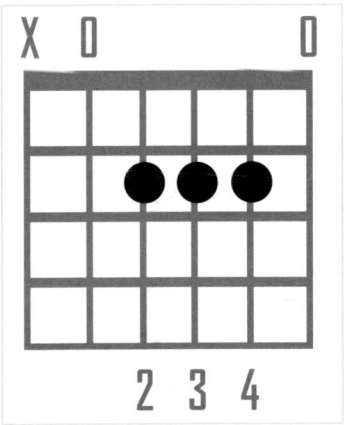

A major

A major

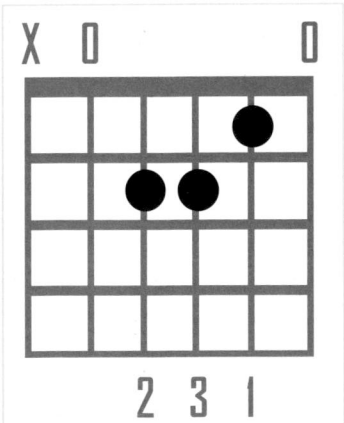

A minor

A minor

Special effects

There are several techniques you can use to use to create different effects when you are playing scales, soloing and **improvising**.

Bending and slides

Bending strings is a technique that is used across all styles of music. This involves pushing, or 'bending', a string so that it plays a higher note.

Slides are a way of getting from one note to another on the same string with a sliding sound effect. You can slide up and down between two notes.

Bending

Play a note using your third finger on the fret, with the other fingers behind it.

Push all your fingers up so they bend the string, making the note sound higher.

Slide

Play a note using your third finger on the fret (although any finger can be used).

Slide the finger towards the guitar's body by two frets to play a note a tone higher.

Hammer ons and pull offs

These techniques can be used to give you very smooth-sounding phrases when playing solos on the guitar. Hammer ons require a little bit of force to sound the second note correctly, but they will get easier with practice. Pull offs are the opposite to hammer ons. You can combine the two techniques into a loop, so that a whole string of notes can be made with just a few picks.

Hammer on

Play a note using the first finger on the fretboard.

'Hammer' down a finger two frets nearer the guitar's body to play a note a tone higher.

Pull off

Place your third finger on the fretboard with your first finger placed two frets down.

Play the first note and pull the third finger away quickly to sound the second note.

Rhythm and chord skills

Once you have mastered the basic skills for chords, you can use further techniques that will help you to put chords together to make sequences and to write songs.

Finger style

Classical, folk and blues guitarists often use their fingers instead of a plectrum. This allows them to play more than one note at once. It also makes a softer sound as they use the fleshy part of the fingertips rather than a plectrum.

Arpeggiating

When you are playing chord sequences, you can strum them in a rhythm, or you could break up the notes in the chord and play them in a sequence. This is called arpeggiating. You can make you own chord sequences up for arpeggiating, too. Play the notes slowly and make sure you let each one ring out.

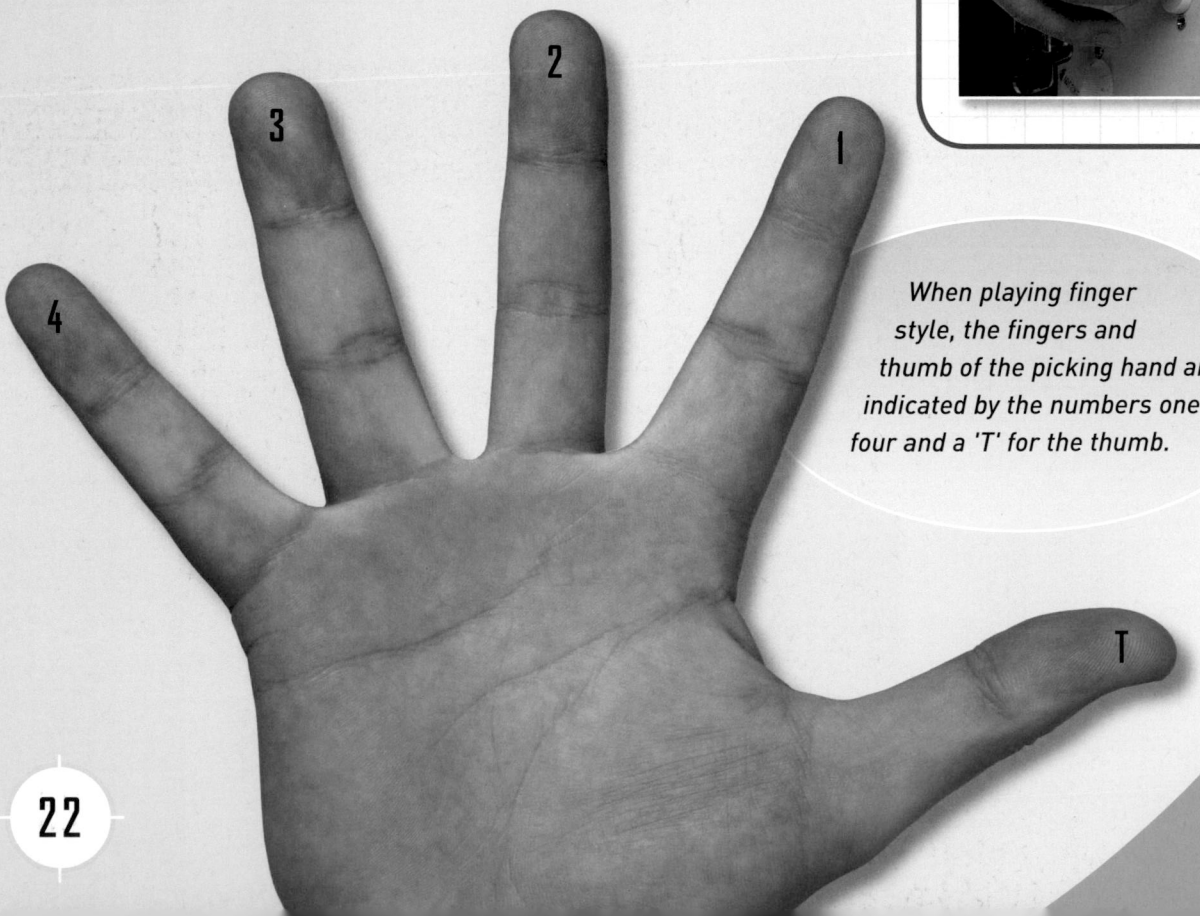

When playing finger style, the fingers and thumb of the picking hand are indicated by the numbers one to four and a 'T' for the thumb.

Finger style sequence

The guitar tab on the right shows a simple arpeggiated chord sequence you can play using **finger style**. The numbers on each string refer to the frets used on that string, while the numbers and letter 'T' along the bottom tell you which finger to pick the string with.

```
e |---------|---------|---------|
b |-------1-|-------1-|---------|
g |-----2---|-----0---|-------0-|
d |---2-----|---2-----|-----0---|
a |-0-------|-3-------|---2-----|
e |---------|---------|-3-------|
  |-T-1-2-3-|-T-1-2-3-|-T-1-2-3-|
     A minor    C Major    G major
```

Using a capo

The guitar capo is a useful tool because it clamps across the six strings of the guitar and allows you to play any open chords but in a different key. This can be very handy if you write your own songs or sing someone else's, but find that the key is too low or high for your voice.

You can move the capo up and down the fretboard in order to find a pitch that best suits you.

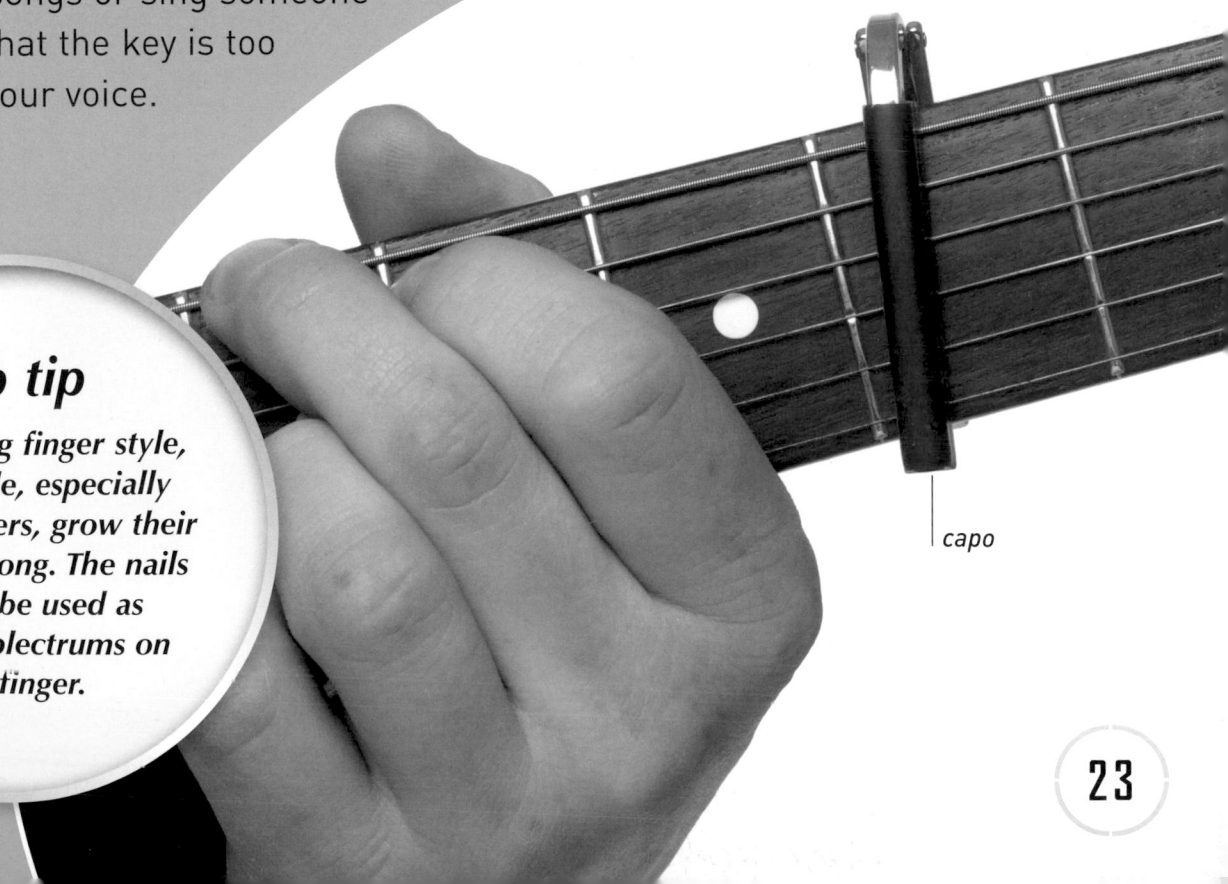

Top tip

When playing finger style, some people, especially classical players, grow their finger nails long. The nails can then be used as individual plectrums on each finger.

Advanced techniques

The techniques shown here will take some time to get right, but mastering them will let you play songs in many different styles.

Tuning variations

Many guitarists choose to change the way their guitars are tuned and then combine this with other techniques to create individual sounds. Drop D tuning, for example, involves tuning your thickest string down from an E to a D. You will need your electric tuner for this, or you could try playing your fourth or D string and tuning the string down to 'match' it (although it will need to be an octave lower). Once you have tuned the string, you can play the three low strings all together. They will make a low, 'heavy' sounding chord. You can then try this on the fifth fret and the third or any other fret of your choosing giving you some more drop D '**power chords**' (see page 25).

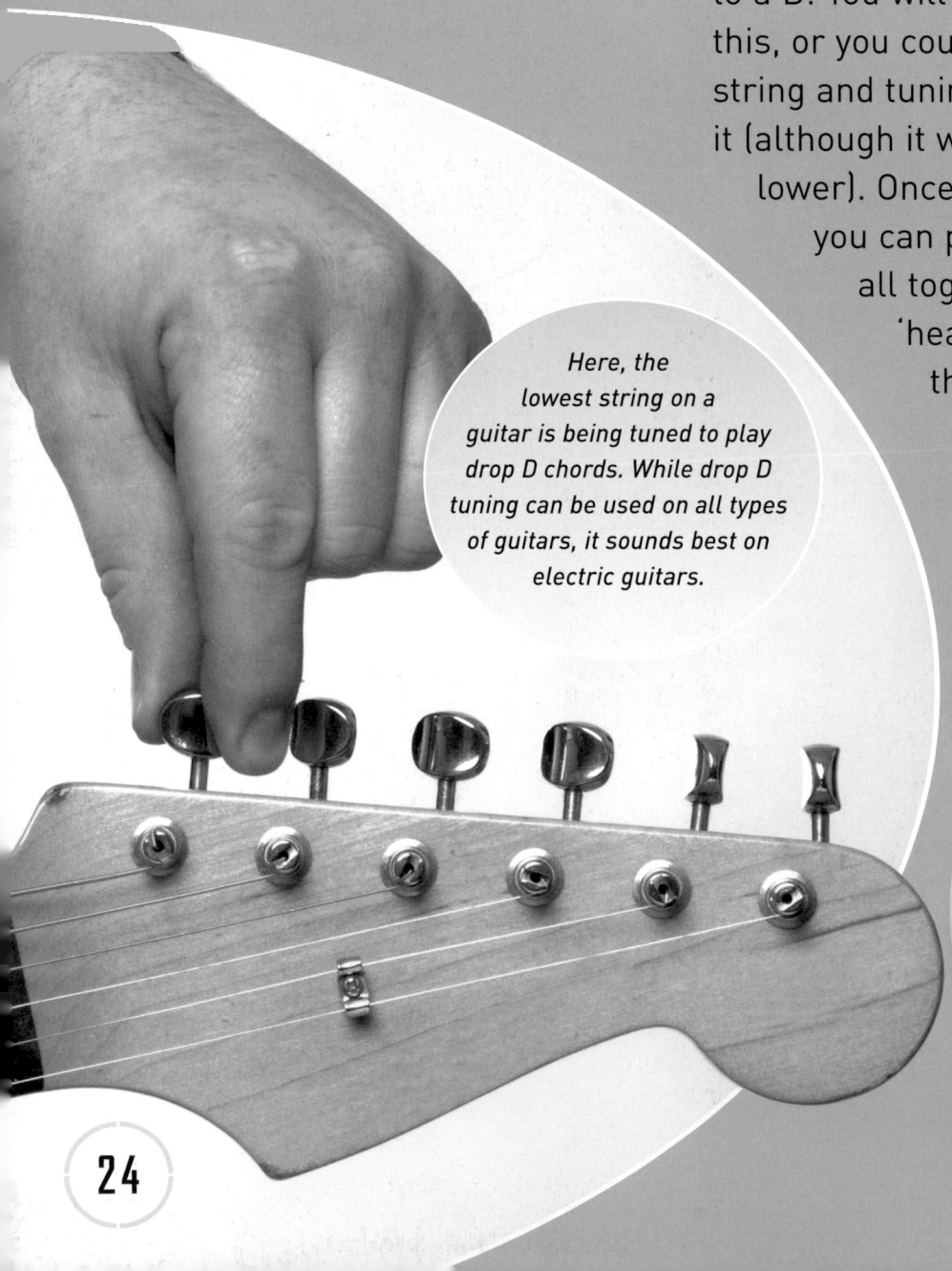

Here, the lowest string on a guitar is being tuned to play drop D chords. While drop D tuning can be used on all types of guitars, it sounds best on electric guitars.

Top tip

Try drop D chords by fretting the lowest three strings on the first, second and third frets. Bands such as the Foo Fighters use this technique for heavy rock songs to great effect.

Harmonics

A harmonic is a chime-like note that sounds different from normal guitar notes. It is produced by lightly touching the string, but without actually fretting a note. This does not work on all frets on the guitar, so you need to know which ones to use. The twelfth fret gives you the best and clearest harmonic (see right), although the fifth and seventh frets will also work.

There are also harmonics available on the third and ninth frets, but these are much harder to master. When they are done correctly, you should hear the chime-like sound. Try this on all the six strings on the twelfth fret, then the fifth and seventh frets, too.

Playing harmonics

Place your second fingertip on top of the twelfth fret of the thickest string.

Pick that string with a firm downstroke using your plectrum and let go of the string with your fret hand as you do so.

Power chords

Power chords are used a lot in rock and heavy metal music. They are simple to do and can be moved around into different positions almost anywhere on the fretboard to make 'riffs' or songs. Bands such as Green Day have used this technique effectively in their songs.

B power chord

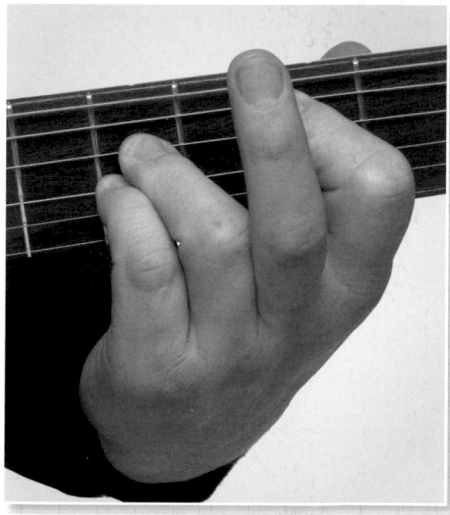

D power chord

Putting it together

In order to write your own songs and play your own solos, you will need to put together the individual skills shown so far. Do not be afraid to experiment – just play what you think sounds good.

Writing songs

By taking some chords and mixing them around, you should be able to come up with chord sequences. Try them in a different order and keep mixing things up. Eventually, you will come across a sequence you like. This can form the basis of your song, over which you can play a melody.

Star file

KURT COBAIN
Grunge guitarist

Born 20 April 1967, Kurt Cobain used the guitar to great effect in his song writing and soloing. He led the band Nirvana during the late 1980s and early 1990s and was also partly responsible for the birth of grunge, a type of music influenced by punk, heavy metal and indie rock. Despite his death in 1994, he is still an enormous influence on guitarists today.

Chord sequence

Below are chord boxes and photos showing a simple chord structure: C major, G major, A minor and E minor. You can write chord sequences down, so that other guitarists can play them.

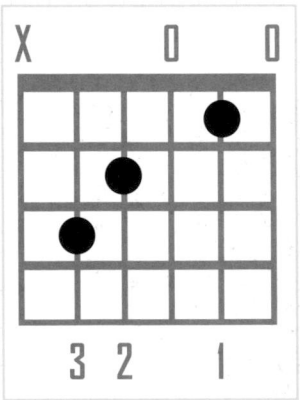

C major

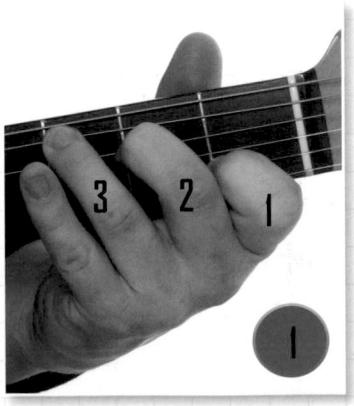

C major

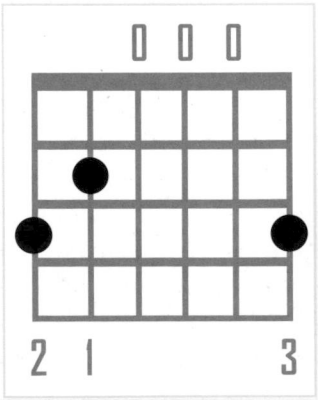

G major

G major

By playing with someone else, you can take it in turns playing the chords and the melody. This informal way of playing is called jamming.

Improvising

Many rock guitarists improvise, or make up, guitar solos during a performance. Improvised guitar solos normally use a scale and change the order and way in which the notes are played. See if you can play the notes from the C major scale shown on pages 14–15 so that they sound good with the chord sequence shown below. There is no right way to play a guitar solo, so just experiment and see what you like, but make sure you have fun!

The chord sequence shown below would look like this: ||:C,,,|G,,,|Am,,,|Em,,,:||
The commas show how many times the chords should be played and the dots at the start and the end show that the whole sequence should be repeated.

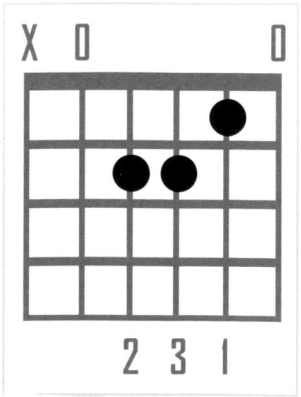

A minor

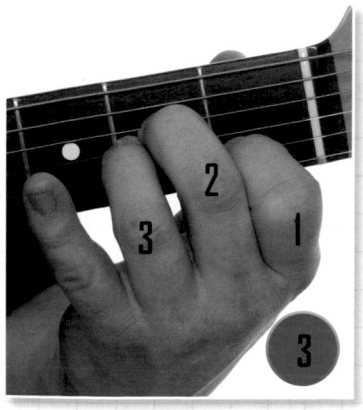

A minor

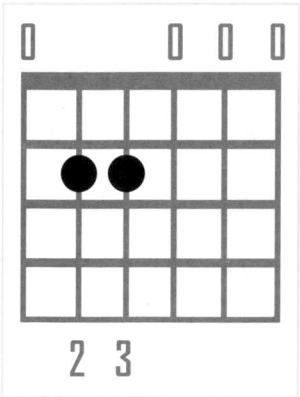

E minor

E minor

Taking it further

With the help of a good music teacher, you can really learn how to master the guitar. Playing with others is also a great way of improving your guitar skills. You may even go on to form your own band and possibly play gigs.

A good guitar teacher will show you correct playing techniques in either one-on-one or group lessons.

Finding a teacher

Your school or your local music shop are good places to ask about a suitable guitar teacher. Shops and schools will have the details of local teachers and will be able to tell you if they teach the type of music you are interested in. Some teachers may give lessons only in classical music, for example, while others might teach rock and blues. However, there are teachers who will cover a bit of everything and are not limited to just a couple of styles.

The Internet is also great for locating a music teacher near you. It can also be a good source of guitar information, such as tabs and advice on buying guitars and different techniques.

These guitarists are jamming. Many of the biggest bands started out with a group of friends playing for fun, just like this.

Playing with others

Working with other musicians is a very important part of guitar playing. You should be sympathetic to other musicians and make sure you always listen to what other people are playing. If you enjoy playing with other people, you might want to think about forming a band and even playing some live gigs. Listen to other guitarists in action and see if you can buy any sheet music of their tunes. Learning what chords and melodies they use could help you to write your own songs. Spend enough time mastering the guitar and you could end up playing it professionally.

Turning pro

To play the guitar for a living, you will have to spend many hours mastering all of its techniques. However, there are plenty of jobs available for professional guitarists. These include teaching music and guitar, working in recording studios and writing your own music.

Glossary

amplify to make something louder.
acoustic in music, acoustic instruments do not need electric equipment to make their notes. An acoustic guitar does not use pickups or an amplifier.
bass lower notes.
clef the symbol that appears at the start of each line of musical notation. It tells you how high or low the notes are.
crotchet a type of musical note that usually lasts for one beat in a simple bar of music.
finger style plucking the strings with all five fingers rather than using a plectrum.
improvising making up something as you go along.
interval the gap between two notes.
jack the connecting socket in an electric guitar or an amplifier. Leads are plugged into the jacks to link the equipment.
key a musical key shows the system of notes and chords that a piece of music uses as its central note or root. Keys are based on one of the notes (A to G) and can be major or minor.
magnetic field an area in which a magnetic force acts. Pickups on an electric guitar detect the movement of strings in a magnetic field and change these vibrations into notes.
major a type of key that is said to have a happy sound.
minim a type of musical note that is equivalent to two crotchets.
minor a type of key that is said to have a sad sound.
octave the interval between two consecutive notes with the same letter (e.g., from A to A).
oud an historical instrument that had 11 strings and was played like a guitar.
pickups small magnets on an electric guitar that detect the vibrations of the strings and change these vibrations into musical notes.
pitch how high or low a note is.
power chords heavy sounding chords that use the first and fifth notes of a scale. Sometimes the eight note, or octave, is also used to double up the first note.
rhythms how the beats of a piece of music are broken up.
semibreve a type of musical note that is equivalent to four crotchets or two minims.
semitone the smallest interval between notes.
solo when a single musician plays a part of a song while the other musicians accompany them.
time signature the two numbers, one on top of the other, that are written after the clef and show how many beats there are in a bar.
tone an interval between two notes that is equivalent to two semitones.
treble higher notes.
vibrate when something shakes back and forth very quickly.
vocalist someone who sings a piece of music.

Guitar and music organisations

There are several organisations aimed at helping guitarists find teachers, study for exams and offer advice to the young guitar player.

The Registry of Guitar Tutors (RGT) is the world's largest organisation of guitar teachers and provides guitar exams throughout the world.

The Musicians' Union represents professional musicians and also offers advice and guidance for musicians of all ages and abilities.

Rockschool is an organisation set up to provide exams and gradings in rock and pop music. It also provides advice to students and teachers.

Further reading

There are plenty of books available for the newcomer as well as the more experienced guitarist.

A Guitar: The Science of Sound and More Claybourne, Anna (Franklin Watts, 2008)

Guitar Girl Manning, Sarra (Hodder Children's Books, 2003)

How to Write Songs on Guitar: A Guitar Playing and Song Writing Course Rooksby, Rikky (Backbeat Books, 2000)

The Ultimate Guitar Tutor: A Comprehensive Guide to Learning the Acoustic or Electric Guitar Fleming, Tom (Faber Music Ltd, 2007)

Websites

The Internet is a great place for information on techniques and advice, as well chatrooms to exchange chord sequences and tabs.

guitarteacher.com

A website with free online lessons, videos, tabs and downloads.

www.guitar.com

A guitar network site where you can create your own webpage and swap information with other guitarists around the world.

www.ultimate-guitar.com

One of the world's leading sources of guitar tabs and chords. It contains an enormous archive with more than 250,000 tabs to download.

Index

acoustic guitar 6, 7, 10
advanced techniques 24–25
alternate picking 14
A minor scale 15
amplifier 7, 9
arpeggiating 13, 22, 23

bar beats 17
bending 20
buying a guitar 7

capo 23
chord boxes 13, 19
chord sequences 26–27
chords 12–13, 19, 22–23
Clapton, Eric 5
classical guitar 5, 10
C major scale 15, 27
Cobain, Kurt 26

Drop D tuning 24

Edge, The (David Evans) 15
electric guitar 7, 11, 24
electric tuner 9, 17, 24
E major chord 13
equipment 8–9, 23

finger style 22, 23
fretboard 6, 7, 11
frets 6, 7, 12, 13

guitar heroes 5
guitar solos 27

hammer on 21
harmonics 25
Hendrix, Jimi 5, 8
history 5
holding the guitar 10–11

improvising 27
Internet 28
intervals 18, 19

jamming 27, 29

key 13, 23

leads 9
left-handed players 4

major chord and scale 19
major key 13
May, Brian 5
minor chord and scale 19
minor key 13
musical alphabet 16, 18–19
musical notation 16–17, 18, 19
musical styles 4, 5
music stand 8

octave 18
open string 13
oud 5

picking 14
pickups 7, 9
pitch 6, 23
plectrum 8, 12, 14
power chords 24, 25
professionals 29, 31
pull offs 21

Reinhardt, Django 17
replacing strings 14
rhythms 17, 22–23

scales 14–15, 19
sharps and flats 18
sitting down 8, 10
slides 20
song writing 22, 26
special effects 20–21
standing up 8, 11
staves 16
strap 8, 11
strings 6, 13, 14
strumming 12

tabs 15, 18, 23
teachers 28, 31
time signature 17
tones and semitones 18, 19
treble clef 16
tremolo arm 7
tuning 17, 24
tuning keys 6, 7, 9

volume 7, 9